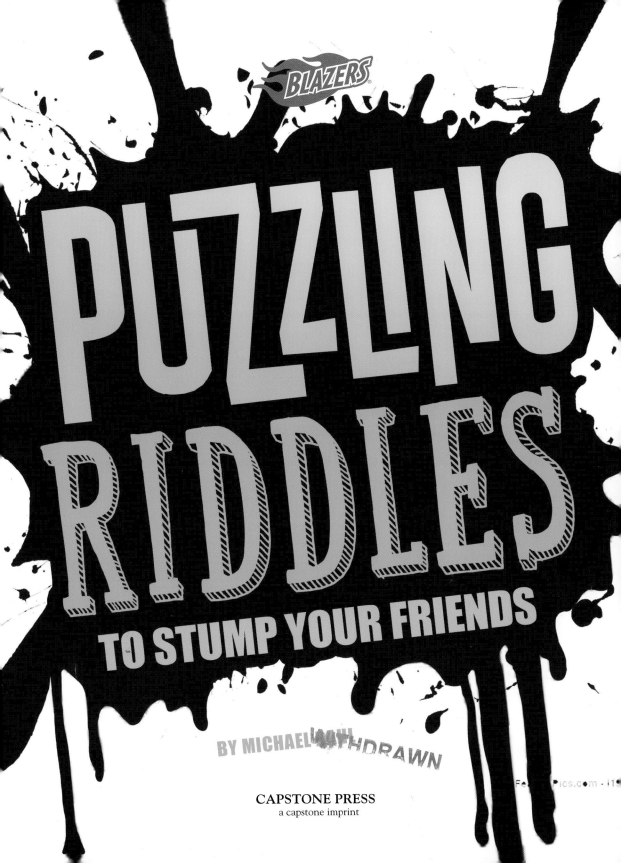

BLAZERS

PUZZLING RIDDLES

TO STUMP YOUR FRIENDS

BY MICHAEL DAHL

CAPSTONE PRESS
a capstone imprint

Blazers Books are published by Capstone Press,
1710 Roe Crest Drive, North Mankato, Minnesota 56003
www.mycapstone.com

Library of Congress Cataloging-in-Publication Data
Library of Congress Cataloging-in-Publication data is available on the
Library of Congress website.
ISBN 978-1-5435-0339-5 (library binding)
ISBN 978-1-5435-0348-7 (eBook PDF)

Editorial Credits:
Mandy Robbins, editor; Eric Gohl, media researcher; Tori Abraham,
production specialist

Photo Credits:
Shutterstock: Andrey_Kuzmin, 15, Balefire, 29, Bomshtein, 30 (left), evenfh, 20,
EvgeniiAnd, 12 (bricks), Hogan Imaging, 17, Hong Vo, 30 (top), Hurst Photo, 21, Jan
Martin Will, 18, jopelka, 10, Little Perfect Stock, 24, Maksim Shmeljov, 27, Muellek Josef,
9, Nerthuz, 23, nito, 12 (feathers), Offscreen, 8, Photoonlife, 7, PongMoji, 14, Portogas D
Ace, 28, Pro3DArtt, 31, Stockforlife, 11, sumire8, 30 (right), Sundari, 31 (background),
Vacclav, 26, vovan, 22

Printed and bound in the United States of America.
010877S18

TABLE OF CONTENTS

RIDDLES ARE SECRETS

A riddle is a secret with clues. When you tell a riddle, you're sharing the clues. And when you figure out the answer, you can feel your brain growing. No one wants a tiny brain, right? So help your friends and share a riddle!

Follow these tips to get big laughs.

1. **Keep a straight face** when telling your riddle. You don't want to give anything away with your facial expressions.

2. **If your friends are stumped**, give them a clue. But don't make it too easy. You want them to think and figure out the answer.

3. **When you say the answer**, say it clearly and loudly. Make it sound like a surprise! This will probably make your audience chuckle and enjoy it even more!

QUICK QUIZZERS

The most famous riddle is the Riddle of the Sphinx. It asks:

> "What goes on four feet in the morning, two at noon, and three at night?"

Answer: **People!** At the start, or morning, of their lives, people crawl on all fours. At noon, the middle of life, they walk on two feet. At night, in old age, they walk with a cane, which gives them three feet.

1. What has two hands but no arms or legs?

A clock

1. What has a head and a foot but no body?

Your bed

2. What gets wetter and wetter the more it dries?

A towel

3. What has to be broken
before you can use it?
An egg

4. What building has
the most stories?
The library

1. What falls but never breaks?

Night

2. What kind of room has no windows or doors?

A mushroom

3. What is full of holes
but can still hold water?
A sponge

4. What do you call a fish
without an eye?
Fsh

5. What has four legs but
never moves?
A table

PUZZLING POSERS

LEVEL: MEDIUM

1. What two things can you never
eat for breakfast?

Lunch and dinner

2. What can travel around the world
but never leaves its corner?

A stamp

3. Which is heavier, a pound of bricks
or a pound of feathers?

Neither — they are exactly the same!

1. What can you catch but never throw away?

A cold

2. What is at the end of a rainbow?

The letter W

3. People buy me to eat, but don't eat me. What am I?

A plate

1. What is the only question where the answer is never "Yes"?

"Are you asleep?"

2. What word is spelled incorrectly in every dictionary?

"Incorrectly"

3. What can you add to a heavy box that will make it easier to lift?

Holes

4. Who is bigger: Mr. Bigger,

Mrs. Bigger, or their baby?

The baby, because he's a little Bigger

STUNNING STUMPERS

LEVEL: HARD

1. I'm light as a feather, yet the strongest man can't hold me for more than 5 minutes. What am I?

Your breath

2. Poor people have it. Rich people need it. If you eat it you die. What is it?

Nothing

3. What goes around and around a tree, but never gets tired?

The bark

1. No matter how hungry they may be, people in the Arctic will never eat a penguin. Why? **Because penguins live at the South Pole. The Arctic is at the North Pole.**

2. A king, a queen, and two twins all lay in a large room. But there are no grown-ups or children in the room. How can this be?

They are different types of beds.

3. What is as big as Godzilla but doesn't weigh anything?

Godzilla's shadow

1. How many seconds are in a year?

Twelve! January 2nd,

February 2nd, March 2nd ...

Sun	Mon	Tue	Wed	Thu	Fri	Sat
1	2	3	4	5	6	7
8	9	10	11	12	13	14
15	16	17	18	19	20	21
22	23	24	25	26	27	28
29	30	31				

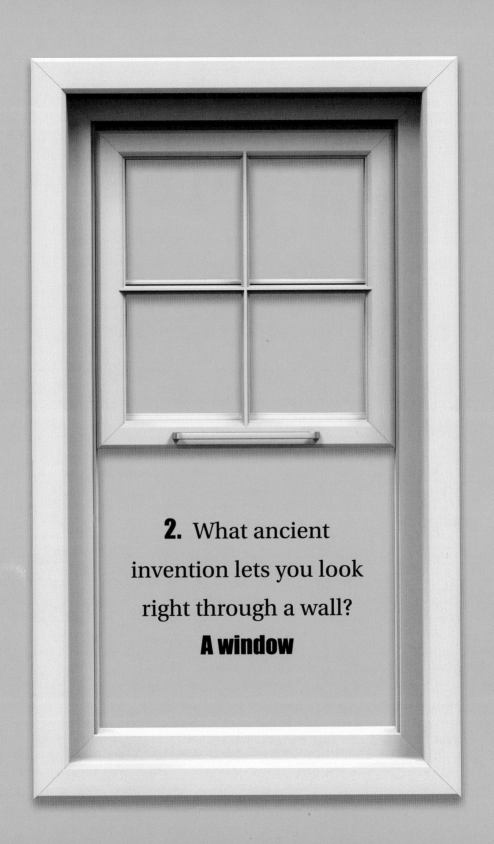

2. What ancient invention lets you look right through a wall?
A window

BOGGLING BRAIN-BUSTERS

LEVEL: GENIUS

1. Willie's mother has three children. The first is named April, the next is named May. What's the name of the third child?

Willie of course!

2. A cowboy rode into town on Friday. He stayed in town for three days and rode out on Friday. How was that possible?

Friday was the name of his horse.

1. Mr. Blue lives in the blue house.

Mr. Pink lives in the pink house.

Mr. Brown lives in the brown house.

Who lives in the white house?

The president

2. A boy was rushed to the hospital. But the doctor said, "I cannot operate on this boy. He is my son!" Yet the doctor was not the boy's father. How could this be?
The doctor was the boy's mother.

3. A truck driver is going in the opposite direction of all the vehicles on the street. But the police don't stop him. Why?
He is walking.

1. You are in a dark cabin. You have only one match. There is a newspaper, a lamp, a candle, and a fireplace. Which should you light first?

The match

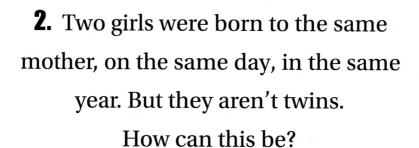

2. Two girls were born to the same mother, on the same day, in the same year. But they aren't twins. How can this be?

The girls are two members of a set of triplets!

3. What starts with T, ends in T, and only has T in the middle?

A teapot

1. Grandma is knocking at the door. She's come for breakfast, but you forgot! You have a jar of peanut butter, a jar of jam, and a bag of bread. What do you open first?
The door — let Grandma in!

2. A man was outside walking in the rain. He didn't have an umbrella, a hat, or a raincoat. His clothes and shoes got soaked. But not a hair on his head got wet. Why?
He was bald.

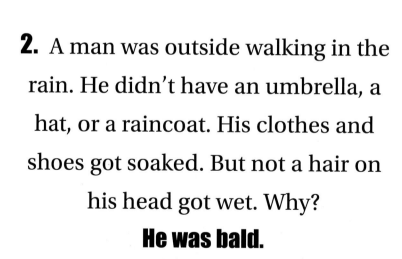

3. Where can you find a microwave?

On a teeny, tiny beach!

READ MORE

Elliot, Rob. *Laugh-Out-Loud Road Trip Jokes For Kids.*
Laugh-Out-Loud Jokes For Kids. New York: HarperCollins, 2017.

Lewis, J. Patrick. *Just Joking: Animal Riddles.* National Geographic
Kids. Washington, D.C.: National Geographic, 2015.

Yoe, Craig. *LOL: A Load of Laughs For Kids.* New York:
Little Simon, 2017.

INTERNET SITES

Use FactHound to find Internet sites related to this book.

Visit *www.facthound.com*

Just type in 9781543503395 and go.

 Check out projects, games and lots more at
www.capstonekids.com

31901061142503